Not Carved In Stone

ELLEN GODFREY

Order this book online at www.trafford.com
or email orders@trafford.com

Most Trafford titles are also available at major online book retailers.

Printed in the United States of America.

ISBN: 978-1-4269-6812-9 (sc)
ISBN: 978-1-4269-6813-6 (e)

Trafford rev. 08/02/2011

 www.trafford.com

North America & international
toll-free: 1 888 232 4444 (USA & Canada)
phone: 250 383 6864 ♦ fax: 812 355 4082

The Lion's Tale

Living so wild in old Innistanglee
Was Morna the Shadow, the thief of Crag Sea.
This lionheart lass, once a princess, 'tis told
Did rob dame and gentleman's jewels and gold.

The child of King Aldred, she fled far away
When one bonny morning her father did say,
"Dear Morna, I feel I should make you a nun
And pass on my kingdom to some future son."

No son ever came to the king and his queen
Who pined til she died at how thoughtless they'd been.
Oh, where was his daughter, the child Aldred reared?
One day ten years hence, he himself disappeared.

In Black Raven Tavern the thief came to sup
On a good hearty meal with strong ale in her cup.
A woman came in and with Morna did sit
And told her she wanted to talk for a bit.

"They call me Old Meggie, my gift is the sight,
A magical vision, a wizard's delight.
I know well your fame and see through your disguise
For I look at you, Princess, through magical eyes.

I come with dire news of your father the king;
You've heard how he's vanished, a most dreadful thing!
I know where he's hidden; it's not far at all.
You, only, can save him from death's ugly pall.

Viana the witch placed him under a spell;
On the Isle of the Ruins the king lies unwell,
All sickly and ravaged, but by Great Orion,
He's guarded, I see, by a magical lion.

Now you and this lion must battle to death
Til one of you gives up your last dying breath;
And then, only then, will King Aldred be freed-
You owe him this, Princess, for your selfish deed."

Old Meggie and Morna set off on the morrow
To save the poor king from his sickness and sorrow.
In Meggie's small boat the two women did sail
To a battle in which it seemed Morna would fail.

The Isle of the Ruins they reached in a day
And on this lush island pure magic held sway.
They tied up their boat to a young willow tree,
"Poor Morna," said Meggie, "God's speed unto thee."

Into the willows, the ash, oak and vines,
The ferns and the cypress and ivy-rope twines,
The grandest stone ruins peep here and hide there
The largest one beckons, "Come in if you dare."

Drawing her sword Morna tiptoed inside.
So many places for lions to hide!
And where was her father? She looked for him hard
Until she stepped into an ancient courtyard.

"Sweet Morna! My child!" a man's voice did ring-
For there in the courtyard sat Aldred the king!
But there at his side his great guardian lay
Til rising and stretching he padded her way.

Magnificent beasts live all over the world,
But none so majestic as he, thought the girl.
All golden of mane, fur, and amber of eye,
The King of the Beasts seemed to breathe a sweet sigh.

All silken spun gold was the mane of his head-
This beautiful creature soon had to be dead!
"Strike now!" cried King Aldred, "by the Almighty Lord,
Let love be your weapon and not just your sword!"

The thief raised her sword and the battle began.
Oh, no fiercer battle between beast and man!
They slashed, gouged and tore, laid bare bone and ran through,
Their blood stained the ground and the hair and fur flew.

At last with her sword, Morna blinded one eye
Of the lion who let out a terrible cry.

Retreating, exhausted and gasping for breath
The lion withdrew to await welcome death.

"Oh Morna! My daughter! Oh, glorious eve!
You broke the enchantment; now I'm free to leave!"
The king's joy then faded toward the victory won.
"I still feel my throne should be left to a son."

"Begone, then, foul father, you ungrateful cur!
Since Mother is dead then why don't you join her?
I've risked life and limb and have spilled half my blood
To battle a king who truly was good!"

Morna turned on King Aldred and staggered away
Til she came to the place where the King of Beasts lay.
Before him the thief knelt, contrite and in tears,
He still could have killed her, but pricked up his ears.

"Forgive me, my lord, for my injuring you.
I've blinded and maimed for a king so untrue;
If you wish to slay me, I'll not run away,
Accepting my punishment, here I shall stay."

With piteous moan, with one mournful eye,
The lion beheld her, just wishing to die.
She touched him and wondered, "Can his wounds be fixed?"
When his blood and her blood together were mixed.

What magic then happened, one can't rightly say.
But what transformation occurred on that day!
A woman one moment, a lioness the next
And no sweeter way could there be to be hexed.

She hunted his food and she helped him grow strong-
With true love to guide one, how can one go wrong?
The king and Old Meggie sailed back o'er Crag Sea
But the king found no welcome in Innistanglee.

Now Morna does rule with her king at her side,
Once desperate thief, now the King of Beasts' bride.
Princesses and princes are born every spring-
Oh, long live Queen Morna and long live her king!

*

To My Grandmother

With your inspirations born on a wrought iron and glass-top table
You planted within me the need to put pen to paper
And do more than doodle in the margins.
You brought forth a New England as it was
And still should be.
You brought an age gone by back to us
And made us wish we had been there to bear witness.
Your lushly green descriptions painted vivid pictures for all who read you.
Over the radio you helped convince nineteen-thirties America
They should want to walk some distance for a certain cigarette.
But you preferred to talk of our hometown
And what it was like to grow up there when you did.
You taught me to walk in your footsteps;
To put into my own words the world around me-
My perspectives, thoughts and feelings,
My wishes, hopes, dreams and fantasies,
Hoping that Someone Out There would be touched.
I wish you were still here with us,
That I could seek your guidance and glean from your wisdom
All that I could learn to bring your voice and my own
To all people.

*

The Teacup Lady

We saw her looking down at us.
We thought, "How can this be?
There's no way she could get inside
With no apartment key!"

We didn't recognize her face,
Her robe or bobbed dark hair,
But all she did was look
And sip her cup of tea- and stare.

We ran inside and up the stairs,
We opened up the door-

But the stranger and her cup of tea
Had gone, and came no more.

*

Cinnamon

I'm so roly-poly I can't wash my back or sides.
A multitude of sins is what my lovely fur all hides.
My person has to wash me and to brush me every day.
People say I'm much too spoiled but I always get my way.
Dig out all those cat chews- don't hold back that luscious treat,
Don't dare disappoint me; my face is much too sweet.
You can't say no to my big eyes because I show some fats.
I'm gorgeous and I know it- I'm 'Min,' the Queen of Cats.

*

A Pirate's Bride

The fresh golden thatch of the roof newly-laid
Glows brightly against a blackening sky.
The dark bank of stormclouds gloriously staid
By last rays of sunlight which dazzle my eye.

The hills all around us shine emerald green,
Beneath the sheer cliffs roars a sapphire sea.
Our rosebush sports rubies, the brightest I've seen,
A more jewel-studded day there just couldn't be.

My Brendan comes up, slowly hitching along,
He kisses my cheek and toys with my locks,
But hard is his glance 'neath his brow so strong
As he scans the horizon, the ocean, the rocks.

Dear Brendan, past fifty and shows every year
(My twenty-fifth birthday I still have not seen)
He once was a captain, a fierce buccaneer
But wisely took pardon from our king and queen.

With fortune ill-gotten he purchases this land,
He courted and won me and took me to wife

Then built this sweet cottage all by his own hand
To lead a much quieter life.

Now three children later he's still at my side,
A dear, doting father, my love and my friend.
My family still calls me 'our pirate's bride'
Their good-natured teasing will ne'er see an end.

"A strong one a-brewin'," says Brendan at last,
"And I feel it down in me breastbone-
The scoundrels I sailed with not long ago past
Will come back to claim what they think is their own.

The Omen's what we called our ship,
Ye've heard me tell before
We bathed in blood from heel to hip
On that fine man o'war!

They were all rippin' mad when I said I'd retire,
But ere they all went their ways
They called me a coward, betrayer and liar
And they'd be back one of these days.

Aye, one of these days when a bad storm blew in
My portion they'd be back to take,
My rightful portion I'd fought so hard to win!
They'd return and leave naught in their wake."

"What nonsense, dear," I had wanted to say.
"For they are all drunk, hanged or gone!"
But never before has he spoken this way
So I quietly tell him, "Go on."

The wind has come up and the sun has gone down.
A lightning bolt tears through the sky;
It pierces fat stormclouds which grumble and frown
And shedding great teardrops, they cry.

Our eyes are drawn far out to sea-
Once more the lightning flares
And shows a ship not seen by me
Which down upon us bears.

She flies the skull and hourglass against a banner black.
"It's the Omen!" Brendan cries, his big hand pinching so.
"Those mangy dogs! The stinking scum! They have indeed come back!
Inside the house, Celina! Get the children! Go Below!"

I hesitate to leave his side. How could I leave my friend
And let him face an angry mob with which he stands no chance?
"I'll stay and help you fight," I plead, "I'll stay until the end-"
He whirls upon me fiercely, "This is no time for romance!"

He heaves me toward the doorway, I stumble on inside.
I think I hear the shouts of men coming up the beach.
I crouch beneath a window and in this safe spot I hide
And feel inside a cupboard for the gun within my reach.

Scrambling up the long beach path
Fourteen, fifteen men?
Through our herb garden cut a swath,
The shouts begin again!

"We found ye, Cap'n! Said we would!
We got a score to settle!
To 'ide from us ye never could-
Let's see some precious metal!

And where's Celina, you old dog?
Wot's married life been like?
Ye killed 'er, eh, like some old 'og,
I'll bet me marlinspike!"

These men were ghosts, not flesh and blood,
No tissue and no bone-
A gun against this misty flood?
We're truly on our own!

No pistol and no sword need we to make this rabble run.
I fumble through my chest of drawers and pull out what I need,
A weapon more effective than any sword or gun-
I wield it now in battle, though it cannot make one bleed.

Pale wraiths surround my Brendan to smother out his life.
I ready my good weapon and advance upon them all.

A battle 'tween fifteen ghosts and one seaman's wife!
I uncork my vial and let the precious droplets fall.

"Begone!" I scream and cross myself, then at them do the same.
The wails, the shrieks, the caterwauls, the damned, despairing cries!
I see the one called Shanty Joe who rendered Brendan lame.
There one moment, gone the next, a swarm of misty flies.

Gone our adversaries; it's my love, the storm and me.
I help him to his feet and press him tightly to my breast.
"Is it time for romance now?" I ask him solemnly.
"For it's the life of pirate's bride I've come to love the best."

Those sky-blue eyes gaze into mine.
"How did you make them go?"
"Always trust in love Divine,"
As now the vial I show.

He smiles. "I've served with gallant men-"
He gently takes my hand,
"but I'll tell ye once and once again,
At sea or on the land-

I've seen no man with half yer brass
With half yer guts and grit.
Ye're worthy as a pirate, lass,
Be bloody proud of it!

And Sunday off to church I'll go
And be right by yer side-
That way everyone will know
That ye're me pirate's bride!"

To sprinkle all around our place
With holy water pure
Whene'er a stormcloud shows its face
My Brendan's always sure.

*

The Illusion

The ship jungle-gym is nearly done,
Good ship "Illusion", stout and true!
We built it all for Josh, our son
With cabin, mast and cannons too.
The finishing touches fall to me,
To fasten the riggings, unfurl the sails.
I fancy I can smell the sea
On the fine south wind that now prevails.
The seagulls' cries, the ocean's spray,
A pitching ship beneath my feet,
A tide which carries us away
From dock and wharf, from seaport street.
We hoist the colors into the blue,
My salty pirate crew and I!
They swab the deck, I keep a view
Astride my cabin roof so high.
There comes a cry from our lookout hale,
"Navy ships off starboard bow!"
They always come when we set sail…
We'll have to fight them here and now.
We start exchanging cannon fire,
We find our mark again and again,
A lucky shot from them goes higher
And falls on us like evil rain.
I tumble from my cabin top
And fall into the sea.
My breath I catch, my brow I mop-
My family's staring down at me.
"Dad, you OK?" "My heavens, Jack!"
But it's my turn to stare,
For painted there across the back
The name, "Illusion" raises my hair.

*

Memoriam

You left us five years ago tonight.
If only I had known
That would be the last time I would
see you.
At the dinner table you seemed your old
self
With your less-than-perfect singing
And your wonderful outbursts of laughter!
You were born near the end of the Jazz Age
And somehow it painted you with its giddy color,
It infused you with its mood
And its music, even if you couldn't carry a tune.
You made this bookcase I'm using for a desk.
How could we know you were getting ready
to leave?
Five years haven't eased my pain
Or dried a single tear.
But when I see Navy planes in tight formation,
When I smell freshly turned garden earth,
And when on the radio you send us your Big Band songs,
Then I realize how very near you still are to us.
Would you sing to me one last time?

*

Coquina Bay

There to greet a sleepy sun
Which rose reluctantly,
To watch it tint the ocean gold
We climbed the highest dune,
The slumbering town, Coquina Bay
Begins to stir and wake
With orange sunlight in its eyes,
Light breeze to pet the palms.
Such sweet change from city life,
To live, not just exist;
To drink the orange sunrise in

Is breakfast for the soul.
The seabirds dance upon the waves,
We hopscotch through the shells
That strew the shore like Neptune's jewels,
An offering from the deep.
No blaring horns or speeding cars,
No harried workingfolk in sight.
Here a sane and gentle stroll
Will carry us along,
A sun-soaked, citrus-flavored life
Will carry us along.

*

The Old Farmhouse

Against a sky of hammered-iron gray it stands,
Sleeping lilac bushes scratching at its cheeks.
Empty windows stare out like blinded eyes
Vacant, yet still seeing.
Paint the color of old blood, faded by the weather
And shingles fallen like an old man's hair, my hair
Shutters lean askew and the wooden bulkhead door rattles
On loose hinges like chattery dentures.
The old roof is swaybacked, a gaping black wound in its side.
The picket fence leans forward, a row of old walking sticks
Abandoned.
This is no one's home anymore. Or is it?
Is that a cloud moving overhead or…
Smoke from the broken chimney?
Like a bleary eye, asleep too long, opening at last,
A dim orb of light comes to life in an upstairs window.
A breeze I do not feel pulls open the front door
In mute invitation, but I move no closer.
All too much like it was forty years ago
When that door opened to me in welcome.
Now it summons me to face whatever justice
An old farmhouse would bring upon me
For the six deaths I have caused
For money that should have been mine.

I will not go in. Let the mystery so long unsolved
Sleep for another forty years.
No one will ever know- will they?
My only hope is that the old farmhouse will
Speak to no one else
The way it speaks to me.

*

The Surprise Visit

A busier day in Boston no one has ever seen.
I wish I had five dollars for every place I've been.
Paying this and that bill, running to the store,
I stop to bolt a fast-food meal, then off to run some more.

Folks call me a "stay-home Mom," the title doesn't fit.
I wish I could stay home awhile, relaxing just a bit.
My family keeps me running, can't get away from that,
Now it's time to head on home and on my face fall flat.

But as I head to take the train to take me back uptown,
I get a funny sort of urge that makes me stop and frown.
I approach the ticket counter- "One way for Mansfield, please."
I climb aboard and settle back to make the trip in ease.

My Grandma lives in Mansfield; haven't seen her for a year,
I have no need to go there and the ticket price is dear.
I haven't told my family, took no time to make a call,
I've just got to get there, but it makes no sense, that's all.

And fifty minutes later we pull in and make a stop.
Here I am in Mansfield now and off the train I hop.
Do I quite recall the way? I do and start to walk,
I should look for a payphone now but there's no time to talk.

There I am on Church Street way before I realize
My Grandma's not expecting me! Too much of a surprise;
My bag's slung o'er my shoulder as I'm running down the street
What am I even doing here? And oh, my aching feet!

I reach my Grandma's house to find the old front door unlocked.
Is she upstairs? Is she asleep? Don't scare her into shock!

She must be in her bedroom; it's the only light still on.
Why <u>am</u> I here? My family must be wondering where I've gone!

I just set foot inside the house; a voice calls from upstairs,
"Lyssie, dear! Can that be you? The answer to my prayers!"
I run upstairs and find her there, a white and wasted sight.
"I'm too sick to leave my bed, though I've tried since last night."

She couldn't use her phone; it's on a table 'cross the room!
What on earth brought me here to save her from her doom?
"What made you call my name," I asked. "You knew that it was me!"
"I just had to think of you to make you come, you see."

*

Asa Ashby's Tale

This house has stood empty since nineteen-ought-five.
Nobody from back then could still be alive,
Nobody but me, and I'm telling you true,
I shouldn't go in there if I were you.

The Chatwin clan was a decent lot,
The Mister and Missus, George, Maddie and Scott-
The oldest boy, Wendell; he was a bad seed.
Who can say what all drove him in his need?

I was thirteen on that sweet summer day.
Maybe Scott might want to come out and play;
That's when I saw Wendell in front of his gate,
His mouth all a-twitchin', his eyes full of hate.

He never said nothin' just stood there and stared,
I couldn't tell why, but I sure did get scared.
I grinned and said Hey, and he took to his feet
And ran off like lightnin' down Washington Street.

I ran down the walk and I knocked at the door,
Since nobody answered I di'nt knock no more.
I pushed the door open, knew somethin' wa'nt right,
I called out "Hello" and turned on the hall light.

Well, nobody answered; I searched all around,
I smelled somethin' funny but di'nt hear a sound.
A coppery odor, but also like tripe-
I'd walked in a house where trouble was ripe;

Finally I found 'em, the sight raised my hairs;
The Mister and Missus in sitting room chairs,
The boys in their beds, the first room upstairs,
I'd come to a place only seen in nightmares!

Never saw Maddie and that's just as well,
Sheriff said that was a scene out o' Hell.
The pickaxe was found on the floor near her feet,
Out back in their smokehouse- he'd turned her to meat.

Well, sir, nobody saw Wendell no more
Not since that day when he stood near his door
A-lookin' like Satan, that hate in his eyes.
He got clean away, ain't that a surprise!

Well, I swear by my life, and a long one it's been,
No thirteen-year-old should've seen what I seen.
You've heard it said, not from me alone
The devil will always look after his own.

*

The Last Bit of Magic or The Glass Slippers

Just how did they make them? The fit is so fine;
No pinching or binding- the look is divine;
Did they mold them or blow them? Oh, too hard to tell.
They have a soft luster like white, pearly shell.
No bubbles, no seams, imperfections or cracks
And the decorative work- there is nothing it lacks.
These did not cause me to slip or to fall;
They did not make noise when I walked in the Hall.
The bows look like real silk, small studs just like pearls;
The leaves and the vines curve in delicate swirls.
The soft, milky color, the miniscule roses,
The real-looking dewdrops on pretty pink posies.
Never before have I worn such perfection,

I'm sure now to win the young prince's affection.
I <u>must</u> know who made these; Oh, will no one tell?
They are all I have left of last night's magic spell.

*

A Christmas Lament

Friendly snowflake from the sky
Wonders why I sit and cry.
Daddy's lost his job today,
I don't feel like I should play.
Don't know, but I've heard it said
Santa and his toy-filled sled
Don't come to you if you are poor,
Won't fill your stockings anymore.
Mommy can't go out to work;
There's eight of us- no time to shirk.
Daddy's boss is called Mean Joe.
"Downsizing's the way to go!"
That's what he says, but he's not here
To make sure Santa comes this year.
Dad says Mean Joe doesn't care.
I wish I were a millionaire
Then Santa would be sure to come
And bring his joy to everyone.
When I see Mom and Dad so sad
There's no use in my being glad.

*

First Snow

All the land done a virginal veil
And the trees turn out in lacy finery.
The wind whispers low.
The forest murmurs back its answer
While even the birds dare not disturb
The reverent silence.
Waters tinkle beneath an icy muffler

And nature falls quiet in respect,
For this is a holy new season.
Beasts bed down in their thickets
To dream of spring green
As a sugar semiprecious covers
The flowers in their slumber.
Perfect, tiny falling stars appear
To cleanse the air and feed the earth,
Touching us but gently
With purity.
All is readiness for the day
Which never delays,
Which never disappoints.
This season is nature's tribute
To the arrival of the Son.

*

Christmas Craft Show

The sweet, spicy scent as you walk through the door,
Blue tape marking spaces all over the floor.
Shelves, signs and placards, all handmade of wood,
Some mediocre, some very good.
Sweet-scented candles, both beeswax and not,
Packets of dip mix, the mild and the hot,
Racks of doll clothing of all different styles
And racks of dried flowers that go on for miles;
Stained glass suncatchers and fuzzy dressed bears
Handmade scent-soaps free you from your cares.
Dishtowels, potholders, runners for tables,
Machine- and hand-knits with their makers' own labels.
Photograph greeting cards, framed pictures too,
Dough ornaments customized just for you.
Ornaments wooden, porcelain, plaster
Say "Baby's First Christmas" and nothing goes faster!
Birdhouses, lighthouses, slate paintings and such,
Exquisite jewelry costing too much
Bubblebaths, skin care and sweet potpourri,
The loveliest pottery for us to see.

Puppets and poppets and pipecleaner creatures,
Magnets and paperweights are some of the features.
Cute pom-pom critters and cinnamon sticks,
By intricate beadwork some folks show their tricks.
Breathtaking miniatures detailed so true
For your best dollhouse and shadowbox too.
Wooden cat yardsticks that say, "Let it snow!"
All manner of Santas that say "Ho Ho Ho!"
Don't spend all your money; there's still one more stop,
For there's one more table at which you must stop,
Nowhere in the world are there figures like mine,
Completely hand-sculpted and glazed for to shine.
Each signed and dated and no two the same,
All personality, priced without shame.
Even non-Christians come flocking to buy
That special something that catches their eye.
We all love craft shows; we do them each year,
A happy and peaceable time without fear.
They're nutty and frantic and tote-loads of fun-
The Merriest Christmas to everyone!

*

Resumé

Dear Ladies and/or Gentlemen: I had to let you know
Seems like the hundredth time this year my company's let me go
Your ad was in the paper; I couldn't help but see
That you need someone versatile on your machinery.
Well, here I am; I've done it all, a true Jill of all trades
I'll never disappoint you all or rain on your parades.
Never late and never out, attendance records shine
A stronger, better work ethic you'll never find than mine.
I've cleaned toilets, I've mopped floors and worked with auto parts,
A hundred little jobs most gals avoid with all their hearts.
Medical devices, setting stones, security
There couldn't be a single job you couldn't teach to me!
Handpainted badges, jewelry, and pieces the stuff together
I've stood out in the rain and snow, all kinds of nasty weather.
I've lifted hoods and bedliners, made up instruction books

But there's no escaping supervisors' dirty looks.
A cashier in a dimly-lit but psychedelic store
I wondered when I'd see the cops- two bongs above the door!
Let me tell you something. Think about it, it's all true.
My situation would be different were this World War Two.
I'd be in very high demand, if you just supposie-
Would I stand a better chance if my first name was Rosie?

*

Welsh Class

I'm looking all around me; no familiar face in sight.
It just figures I would be alone in such a plight.
These people are not foreigners. No, I'm the stranger here.
Across the sea in this strange school, I feel devoid of cheer.
Best by far to learn it and to use it practically
But I just know I'll get an F and- back across the sea!
For all my fellow students this is just "refresher course."
But for me, the foreigner, it's pricklier than a gorse.
I sweat and plug and cram and chew my pens down to their core
I've never eaten so much ink at any time before!
But then the year is over, I wonder if I pass
Until the marks are all made known- I'm top marks in my class!

*

Bengal

I love your beautiful rosettes,
Your spangled, glittered pelt.
It's certainly the finest fur
That I have ever felt.
Such tiger stripes and leopard spots;
Such clouded, marbled waves…
They saw this fool a-comin',
No money shall I save.
You cost a little fortune
Much more than my first car!
But you approached me with a "Mrrr?"

I knew just what you are.
You're such a precious kitty
A leopard to take home,
And I'll give you ten times the love
That you have ever known.

*

Irish Church Ruins

See how the sun comes through
The empty circular window
Making a cross
On the floor inside.
The soft voice of a pan flute
Whispering in our minds' ear,
The song of our centuries
Singing a song of emeralds,
Of green,
The color of faith eternal.
The very stones cannot forget.

*

Oriental Garden

Bamboo drums against itself
In the jade-colored garden.
Giant goldfish like bright handkerchiefs flourished
Back and forth beneath the water
Fed by the tinkling brook.
A wooden footbridge invites me to the other side
To where the flowers grow
And where the birds sing.
No hurries and no worries here, just deep green serenity.
Over there! Are those geishas?
Even their voices are tinkling and sweet
Responding to the notes of a stringed instrument.
The pebbles underfoot are like pearls;
Perhaps that is what they are.

It would not surprise me, for surely this is
A part of Heaven.
Are there geishas in Heaven? Perhaps they are angels
Who are meant to match the décor.
And grandly overhead rise the Twin Pagodas,
Red, a cool green and ornamented with silver.
I sink down onto a wooden bench and drink in
The emerald solitude.
I dream of lovely miniature fountains
And cats waving upraised paws.
I hear the soft, pink and yellow notes of a flute
Or is that some kind of bird?
Suddenly I long to be robed in silk
The color of the gardens all around me.
I wish to have my hair combed, piled high and scented.
Soft footfalls…
"May I get you something to drink?"
Is it one of the geishas?
No; it is a waitress with a cocktail menu.
The placemat of the Twin Pagodas Restaurant
Sits before me as it had
When it inspired my deep daydream.

*

A Love Affair

A beach softly spread with sugar
heals my feet and spirits too
with primitive medicine.
Upon my arrival I feel as one returning home.
A warm and affectionate breeze welcomes me
with its salt-sweet breath, petting and caressing,
wondering where I've been for so long.
The sun paints my skin a deep, piratical brown
and highlights my dark hair with doubloon blonde.
When the tide goes out
the sand under my feet is a thick pudding;
then the beach is a treasure-trove of wondrous creatures
to examine, then release.

It leaves little gifts for me to find;
the sea glass, dropped money, a pretty shell, a piece of jewelry.
Sometimes the sun will play too rough
in its joy to see me
and leave me blistered and sore.
What matter? We're still in love
and have been since my earliest childhood.
What could have been more magnificent than
a fierce storm out over the ocean?
Something out of a storybook with its own lights display!
And I, an eager audience in my front-row seat
in the dunes, treasuring every moment.
Any warnings of jellyfish or sharks are but a minor annoyance
like the big green flies who try to discourage me.
We are in love and not to be discouraged.
It pains me to leave.
I always want to stay forever
and let the beach work its ancient, salty magic
upon a willing spirit.

*

Down Wonder

Deep orange-red as far as the I can see,
Even the air smells different; thicker,
Heavy with the tang of strange vegetation,
Colored by the calls of birds unknown to me.
Most of the way around the world from home,
Yet I could settle here happily
Among this alien flora, fauna and sweet, slow-moving people.
Strange and marvelous sights wait around every corner,
Wishing to be drunk in and digested like an exotic dish.
Don't move too quickly; you'll miss something!
A herd of wild camels stare at me knowing me for a stranger.
Full-bloods and half-breeds squint from their barstools
In the local watering hole
And later that night peer into your tent to get a better idea
Of who you are and where you come from.
In the evening the birds sing me to sleep, extending every

kindness
To one far from home and family.
The stars don't hesitate to shine for me
Like zillions of diamonds on black satin.
The Southern Cross reminds me to have faith
As far as I am from the familiar.
A wandering dingo acts like a puppy to wheedle some 'tucker,'
Even the hideous and gargantuan spider does not chase
Though I have disturbed its web.
The tiny bush flowers go out of their way to burst into bloom
Just to make me smile
And guess at what they might be called.
The dead mulga wood gives off a sweet smoke
When we burn it for our campfires
And lightly scents our clothes, adding its own special seasoning
To whatever we cook; the billy tea or the beer damper,
The pavlova or the Mystery Meat.
You must climb the Rock and revere its time-honored paths
And go quite speechless at the view from on top of the world.
Do you crave some ancient magic?
Digeridoo music as the sun begins its descent
And the sky turns marmalade and deep blue
When the campfires are being lit
And the stories are ready to be told.
Look,
Listen,
And taste the deepest soul of an entire continent
Gathered where you are for that brief moment-
What was lost and buried beneath centuries comes pushing up
To present itself to the sons and daughters of other lands.
Embrace it within yourself, savor and keep it,
For who knows when or if you will find it again?

*

The Ruins of Darkley Wood

'Pray let the wandering soul pass by
O, let no pilgrim stop to spy.
Here in this forest, Darkley Wood

An evil dwelling place hath stood,
A hovel black wherein did dwell
A man who brought back souls from Hell.'

"That's what it says, right on this sign
All overgrown with ivy vine.
We know this sign is very old;
Middle Ages, so we're told.
Some priest carved these words in stone
To mark where this creep had his home.
There's really nothing here to see,
A pile of rocks, if you ask me.
It's historic, on the maps,
A story told on mothers' laps.
Zizrid was the sorcerer's name,
He had one wicked claim to fame.
If someone Less than Good would die
Zizrid of the Bulging Eye
Would cut the corpse with knife of bone
And suck some blood and then sneak home-
Here he'd vomit out the blood
And raise the soul of Less than Good.
Someone killed him, don't know who
I only know that this is true;
They threw him down a long, deep pit
And moved a stone on top of it.
They say it happened; I don't know.
That's just the way the stories go.
There is one thing outside the norm-
None know why the ground's so warm,
Why in October there's a stink,
My Dad says compost fumes, I think.
Sometimes I get the urge to look
The story's told in every book.
Sounds fantastic, I admit.
A real live sorcerer! Think of it!
I've got a project due at school
And this idea that's pretty cool.
Explore the Ruins, write a paper
Describe all aspects of my caper.

Sensational! I'm sure to net
The highest grade that you can get!

With this pipe I'm moving stones
Hear the way it creaks and groans!
I'll put them back, but I must see
If anything remains for me

To write about and get a grade
To put all others in the shade!
The ground right here feels almost hot
And what I smell is not plant rot.
Oh, my God! That awful smell!
What could it be? Who can tell?
That's not compost, that I know
Not from all that time ago.
There's a pit here in the floor;
Going down ten feet or more
With stairs they built right in the wall!
If I went down them, would they fall?
I'll write some more when I get back;
I'll leave these papers in my pack."

(Translated from the archaic script found written in blood on the previous paper):

Who sent this buxom child to me?
Who may I thank for being free?
This juicy wench afforded joy-
A hearty meal for this old boy!
Now I'm free to walk the earth
For my first time since deathly birth!
I know not what the maid hath penned;
No matter! She hath reached her end!

(Notice on the school bulletin board):

This is Constable William Black.
We found some papers in the pack
Of this young lady, Rhonda Bright
Missing for one year tonight.
Investigation's underway,
No traces yet, we're sad to say.
No 'school project' was completed.

This warning now must be repeated!
Stay away from there, we say!
Don't touch a thing; just keep away!
The Darkley Ruins are not safe-
Let no <u>more</u> parents sit and chafe!
For dares, initiations, pranks-
Stay <u>clear</u> of the Ruins, thanks.
On this young lady's whereabouts
Some private citizens have their doubts.
The superstitious ones will say
The evil took Miss Bright away.
Who is the fiend who wrote in blood?
All leads we have aren't any good.

The blood belongs to poor Miss Bright,
That's all the news we have tonight.
Investigations still go on-
We go down in the pit at dawn.
Now for the sake of Rhonda Bright
Missing for one year tonight
Let us repeat the warning told
To passersby in days of old…

'Pray let the wand'ring soul pass by
O, let no pilgrim stop to spy
Here in this forest, Darkley Wood
An evil dwelling place hath stood
A hovel black wherein did dwell
A man who brought back souls from Hell.'

*

From Beyond: A Plea

Won't someone please find me? Don't let me stay here
Don't let me stay down here for hundreds of years.
Though nothing but bones now, I long to find rest.
My family's plot is the place I'd like best.
Won't someone please see me? Oh please find my pack-
I've papers inside it for you to take back.
I've met a bad ending, so scary! So sick!

Old Zizrid's living by some evil trick!
Won't someone please help me? I'm all but picked clean.
I did read the warning; now see what they mean!
I've hurt my poor family; how dumb could I be?
Misfortunes it takes to get people to see!
Zizrid was down here, all dry flesh and bone-
He hit me so hard I fell down on the stone,
Down onto the stone floor where I hit my head
And beat me so badly I thought I'd be dead.
Then with a sharp knife blade he sawed off my hair
And wove it all into a belt he now wears.
He took the same knife blade and then cut my throat
And butchered me, living, like some poor old shoat.
Oh, please, someone find me and take me back home
And lay me to rest in a place I have known.
Oh, Mom, Dad and Devon, I miss you all so!
Stupidity took me away, this I know.
If only I could, I'd come back to you now
And try to make up for my error somehow.
I'd wash all the dishes and scrub all the floors
And wouldn't sneak out of the yard anymore,
All this I'd promise, but know it's too late
Please warn other folks so they won't share my fate.

Watch out for the creep with the blonde braided sash,
He's bony and has a complexion like ash.
Oh, please, someone find me and let me find peace
And bring me back home so that I'll find release.

*

Candy House 2004

Come in and try my tasties, dears, come in and don't be shy.
I've biscuits and I've pasties, dears, and luscious cherry pie!
Come in and don't be frightened, dears, don't mind that pile of
bones.
Last night Grammie's tummy was upset by Alice Jones-
I mean, it's only from a chicken, I'm afraid I ate too fast.
Do try this lovely sucker, dears, the kind that lasts and lasts.

And try my finest gingerbread! It's won a prize before!
Why do you keep on turning, dears, and looking toward the door?
Oh, that's just Grammie's kitty, dears, he wouldn't hurt a fly.
Sit down at the table, dears, and have some apple pie.
Have some whipped cream cake, my dears, and jelly beanies too,
Treacle, trifle, truffle, dears, all here and just for you!
Where <u>do</u> you think you're going, dears? You cannot get thee hence,
For Grammie's just installed a Kids' Invisi-bubble Fence!
You thought that Grammie burnt before, but I tell you with glee,
You cannot kill a Fairy Tale, you Hansel/Gretel wanna-be!

*

Gone

Still feel your kiss upon my cheek…
We've not been married one full week.
A little purple bear, keepsake
In the fridge some wedding cake.
On my finger, band of gold
Notes you wrote me, feeling bold.
Few fragile dreams to build upon
Bring no comfort now you're gone.
Once you made me your new bride,
Didn't know you'd run and hide.
You used to use the word Forever
Now I'm thinking you meant never.

*

Nightmare

No one is wearing a smile today. Daddy was in a bad mood;
He and Mom seemed very tense. He didn't touch his food.
They always tell me, "Eat breakfast!" But Dad didn't eat his today.
Mom seemed to want him to stay at home, but he went to work anyways.
I didn't want to say anything. I don't know what this is about.
Mom is already shaky; I don't want to cause her to shout.
This is my summer vacation, but Mom says I can't leave the yard.
There's no one to play with in this neighborhood, so having fun's

awful hard.

People were fighting on TV last night, they scream on the radio too.

Daddy and Mom just turned them both off and told me, "It's bed-time for you."

Everyone's acting all crazy! Shoppers are crowding the stores!

People are carrying posters outside showing people all covered with sores.

I even saw somebody knock a man down and everyone ran over him!

But my neighbor Isabel led me inside and turned all her lights down dim.

I tried to ask her what's going on but she couldn't or wouldn't tell.

She took a swig from a bottle of "hootch" and said, "The world's going to Hell."

Some people just broke the store window! They're stealing what-ever they touch!

Whatever's wrong with the town and the world, it's gotten to be too much.

I run inside to Mommy and- what's that wailing sound?

She grabs my hand and screams, "We've got to get underground!"

She pulls me toward the cellar (test pattern on TV)

We run down cellar- one bright flash- is all that we can see.

We huddle in a corner and Mommy starts to cry.

"You're only seven, Johnny; that's too young to say goodbye."

Whatever Mommy means by that, don't think I want to know.

But if this isn't some bad dream, who will make it go?

*

Falling Star

Dainty star a-falling: an omen good or ill?

Art thou a message from above? Inform me of His will!

Art thou celestial accident or something meant to be?

An angel falling from his grace, a lesson unto me?

Or art thou gift, a gem from Heav'n, a diamond from the sky?

Portent of danger, rousing me and telling me to fly?

O breathless little falling star! O wilt thou not reveal

Thy purpose and thy mission to this creature as I kneel?

O thou, too quickly gone from sight, no more should I behold
Yet trailing from thy heels is left a sparkling thread of gold.

O faceless, nameless gazer, I plummet to my death.
Thou art surely dazzled by my glorious dying breath.
My time has come, my life is o'er, my years are finally spent.
Farewell, then, o tiny one! I die in my descent!
No more seek me on map or chart, or in thy gazing glass
For we all have time to Be, and then comes time to Pass.
A wondrous time to blaze and shine, then comes time to dream.
The time we spend is ne'er as long as Time would have it seem.
I fall! I fade! I say no more, my death at least is nigh.
One day another star more fair shall take my place on high.

*

Rose Quartz

I'm love and I'm springtime, I'm innocent passion
I'm sweetness and purity, tenderness, truth
I'm friendliness, feeling and always in fashion
I'm goodliness, gaiety, softness and youth.
I'm childlike and vibrant, I'm so full of play
I'm warm and I'm caring, I'm precious and new
All feminine prettiness, lovely as day
If you love these qualities, I love you too.

*

Modern Priorities

Hello, what are you looking at? It seems to be my lunch.
You must like tuna sandwiches, milk and yogurt crunch.
Perhaps my homemade cookie? Is that what interests you?
What's up? You keep on staring, kinda rude, to tell you true.
I gorge on carbs and calories? I'm digging my own grave?
My tuna's full of mercury, the dolphins I must save?
The mayo in my tuna fish is nothing but pure fat?
Too much sugar in my cookie and there's NO forgiving that.
Too many cherry colas like the one I had for break;
Celery sticks and carrots are the snacks I should take.

I should switch my lifestyle, join a gym, go on a diet?
No fats or sugars, carbs or food, I should really try it?
Well…
On your car I see a fish who's sprouting little "feets."
You think that's acceptable, but not my bag of sweets.
You feel a person must be thin in order to be whole?
You're so worried for my body- don't you worry for your soul?

*

Paper Wasp

My home is in an apple tree, that old one by the brook.
It's bigger than a beach ball, man! Come by and have a look!
Come down and meet the family! We'll be glad to see ya,
But the minute you come close, I wouldn't wanna be ya.
We're a major creep-out and we rule the territory.
Have any tried to move us out? Yeah, that's one sad story.
This guy comes with his can of spray and we all see him comin'.
He thinks he's gonna plug us until we all start a-hummin'.
That dude is cold! Not one of us'd even had to sting!
They said it was a heart attack- ain't that the coolest thing!
We're so small compared to you- we scare you into fits!
And if we get inside your cars, you drivers go to bits!
You humans really crack us up! We love to yank your chain!
And when the joke is over we can cause some major pain.

*

Fantasy Convention/ OR Three Days of Magic

The elegance that walks the halls, right out of history books.
The mundane can't believe their eyes; they give us second looks.
Such princesses and cavaliers, the new-age vampire goth,
A pretty other-worldling white and floaty as a moth.
Knights in armor, superheroes, aliens everywhere,
The warriors of Celtic stock with waist-length braided hair,
The smartly-dressed Victorians, the Fairy Folk in green,
Some ancient Greeks and Romans, a medieval king and queen.

Ev'ry rainbow's color you will find within our midst
In satins, brocades, velvet, some with spangles lightly kissed.
Unbelievable the makeup jobs, the jewelry and wigs,
Fine coronets and headdresses, top hats to laurel sprigs.
The hoopskirts and the panniers, the corsets laced with care,
Uncomfortable? Why, not at all! They're selling them upstairs
Next door to where the werewolves are installing resin fangs,
Across from where the armorer's full suit of armor hangs.

Gold-gilt is the ballroom under crystal chandeliers
Where ev'ry different epoch in its finery appears.
And here we gather to the dance; each ball with different themes,
Here ev'ry period intertwines, a myriad of dreams.

In restaurants and hotel bars the staff and patrons stare-
Most with a fascinated smile, some with a sour glare.
A luncheon of executives turns unbelieving eye
On Marie Antoinette and her proud king as they stroll by
Some people ooh and ahh and smile to see us walking 'round;
Some say that to the funny farm the likes of us are bound.
While some will beg for photographs and with us want to pose,
There's always one who shakes his head and wrinkles up his nose.

It's three sweet days of make-believe before the party's done
And back home to our mundane lives we revelers must run.
But we'll be back again next year, you'll see us one and all,
To shed our ordinary ways and have ourselves a ball.

*

Auntie Lil

My Auntie Lil invited me to spend some time with her.
She knows I love the Twenties and it's her house I prefer.
I told her I'd come over and stay perhaps two weeks-
My company laid me off last month, two-bit computer geeks!
As if that wasn't quite enough, my Jim filed for divorce,
He said he found another girl and then took off, of course.
I don't know what on earth caused that. For ten long years he cared-
Now MIA for just a month, off with this girl he's snared.

I tell myself it's not my looks, for they aren't bad at all.
(Perhaps I would be happy now if I had married Paul.)
At thirty still a hippie chick with hair down to my hips,
Hip hugger jeans and sandals, cherry gloss upon my lips.
With time on hand, no offers yet and fit to climb the walls,
I make the drive to Auntie Lil's, those dark and narrow halls.
Lil is really not my aunt; she's Dad's at ninety-three
But looking great and spry and sharp, she could be one to me.
Old Lil's a saint. She hugs me tight and makes me right at home.
Her cooking's great, enough to stop my Jim from nightly roams.
She tells me I'm too thin and should do something with my hair,
She takes me to her guestroom and she settles me in there.
She's such a dear, so sweet and warm; I love her just to death.
In every room there is a ghost of lilac's pretty breath.
Lil puts me right to bed but stops to sit down next to me.
"Life can seem so bitter cruel, but there's still hope, you see.
My poor Lindy," Lily purrs, stroking my long hair.
"You've been through way too much at once that damn right isn't
fair.
Together we will make things right with tender loving care.
For when you love someone it makes your burdens light as air!
Try not to feel to bitter, love, and put yourself above it.
I have a nice surprise for you; I know you'll really love it.
There's nothing like a change to make a woman forget sorrow.
Do try to get some sleep now, pet. We'll fix you up tomorrow.
"I love you, Auntie Lil," I say and give her a hug and kiss.
"I'll fix everything," she says, "my pretty little miss."

I drift to sleep and dream of things that frighten me a bit,
Of handsome men and money, each of whom must take a hit!
In my dreams I see Lil's garden, flowers lush and strong
And wonder why I feel uneasy staying there too long.
At different points all through the night I feel someone is there,
Perhaps it's even more than one; to look I do not dare.
Finally I can take no more and I jump out of bed,
Pull on my jeans and sweater, pull my brush across my head.
A little walk will do the trick; it's what's I've always done
When nightmares and unease conspire to render dreams un-spun.
I tiptoe, silent, from the house. A full moon lights my way
Down a lovely tree-lined street where peace holds blessed sway.

Night walks never frighten me; they bring me relaxation.
They help me go right back to sleep and turn from my vexation.
Off to my left a movement- a shadow? A night bird?
Then I hear the woman's voice; it's one I've never heard.
"Lil Macauley! Shameless thief! I'd kill you here and now-
Take a knife and butcher you and gut you like a cow!
You wicked, evil devil's wench! I know well what you've done!
You've murdered your five husbands and the fifth one was my son!
Black-hearted, scheming Jezebel! You live without a care!
I can't do what you deserve, but I'll pull out your hair!"
And there she stood to block my path, a woman dressed in white-
Though not tall, she looked quite strong and itching for a fight.
I start to say, "That's not my name-" she grabs me by my arm
A pair of pliers would hurt less and do a lot less harm!
She tore my clothes, she punched and slapped, and tore at my poor hair,
I tried my best to fight her back, but it's like punching air!
Finally I broke away and tore back down the street,
I ran inside the house afraid that Auntie Lil I'd meet.
And still outside the house I hear the woman, screaming in her fury,
"Money bought you justice; bought your judge and bought your jury!"
This crazy woman thinks I'm Lil! What do her ravings mean?
I'm just too dazed and start to sob, against the door I lean.
Finally staggering back to bed, I dream uneasy dreams,
Something about murder trials; the people come in streams.
I think I see my Auntie Lil, so young and veiled in black,
She looks a lot like me, I think. I'm taken quite aback.
A lovely 'twenties flapper, all sleek but pale and tragic.
Her wet blue eyes are ringed with kohl and work a kind of magic.

I jolt awake and see no sun but my dear Auntie Lil.
She beams at me, all strong and spry and looking fit to kill.
She puts her finger to my lips and says, "Don't say a word;
I know you met Maude Blaise last night, that nasty looney bird.
I'd hoped that wouldn't happen, but it has, and more's the pity.
We'll go have our breakfast, then we'll start to make you pretty."
As we eat I question her and ask her what this means.
Who was that woman given to making violent scenes?
"Maude Blaise was mother to my Bill. She wasn't very stable.

Swore I killed him, and my life she'd take if she were able.
That cemetery that you saw, the left side of the road
Is full of just such angry folks with souls that bear a load.
That's why I stay clear of it; I rarely venture forth,
Why I never take that road, and only travel north.
Skirt any way around it, but keep clear if you can
For that old boneyard's full of souls who hate me to a man."

Why DO they hate her? Have they cause? I must unravel truth.
Did Lil commit some murders all those years back in her youth?
But she's so sweet and loves me so! How could she ever kill?
How often had she married? And which one was poor Bill?
What does she have in store for me? What's this big surprise?
How will she 'make me pretty?' Some old makeup for my eyes?
I hadn't seen a boneyard; the mist acts like a screen.
And was that the hiding place where mad Maude Blaise had been?
Of course it was; Bill was her son way back in flapper days.
It was nineteen-twenty-four when Lil met Billy Blaise!
So now I'm seeing ghosts, I thought, and have a 'murderess' aunt.
I try to come to grips with this, but find I just can't.

Lil takes me to her dressing room and opens up a drawer
And takes out pale silk underthings she's never worn before.
She pulls out soft silk stockings, a "teddie" trimmed with lace
And such a lovely smile I've never seen upon her face.
She hands the frillies all to me and bids me put them on.
She's searching through her wardrobe for some dress for me to don.
Auntie Lil takes out a gown, an ivory satin dream
All covered with exquisite beads which twinkle seam to seam!
My mouth was hanging open; I just managed, "Auntie Lil"
"It's all for my sweet princess, dear. Now YOU'RE dressed fit to
kill!"
Before you put the dress on, dear, a necessary flair.
Let's step into my bathroom and we'll fix up your poor hair.
We'll do it like I used to do; a simple, basic style."
I felt a little woozy when my long hair hit the tile.
She cut it all off to my chin, then shingled up the back,
Then cut some bangs and shaved my neck. I thought I had to yack.
Lil used some kind of lotion and smoothed it all down sleek.
I'd been too stunned to stop her and now I couldn't speak.
My lips she painted, rouged my cheeks and ringed my eyes with

kohl.
I peered into a mirror and thought, "Mercy on my soul!"
Here was the image in my dreams, the pale and gorgeous Lil
All wicked and all vampy and awaiting a first kill.
"Now let's get this dress on you. You've got some folks to meet.
And wear these pearls, for you are now society's elite!
As lovely as I used to be; too thin, but lovely still.
No Lindy dear, you are the vision of poor old Auntie Lil."

She led me to her garden door, rapped twice and stepped inside.
We descended a short staircase like a groom leading his bride.
She stood me there in front of her at the bottom of the stairs
And seemed to wait for something, idly petting my bobbed hair.
There in the morning mist I saw three figures- four, no, five!
All trying to solidify, but none of them alive.
Five men now stood before us, partly flesh and partly bone.
"My princess, from this moment on, you'll never be alone."
The ghosts advanced upon us and Lil addressed each one;
"Arthur, Byron, Leland, Don- and Billy, my sweet bun!
I've come to keep my promise, pay for murder with my blood,
I killed you all for money, now it's time that I made good.
This is my niece Melinda, my blood flows through her veins.
She loves her poor old Auntie Lil enough to take these pains.
You see she looks just like me, that should be fine for you.
Come forward now and take her, dears, and do what you must do."

Have you ever known a time when the world stopped still?
I must confess that's how I felt at hearing Auntie Lil.
My Auntie the black widow wed and killed five wealthy men
Whom she'd buried in her flower garden, waiting just for then.
"You're still my precious princess, love" Lil tells me with a
kiss.
"I freed you from your troubles, now it's on to Heav'nly bliss!
I cannot face my death just yet; I know it would mean Hell.
Embrace your five new husbands now, my pretty little belle!"
Too scared to scream or try to run, I'm frozen to the spot.
I can't believe what's happening; what hope have I got?
One bony ghost cries, "Skip it, Lil! It's not the girl we want!
It's YOU who's got a price to pay! That's why it's YOU we haunt!"
The ghosts rush forward in a mass; I yelp and dodge aside,
Can't watch whatever happens to the ghosts' unfaithful bride.

I block my ears, don't listen, still I'm weeping at her screams.
I'm praying that I'll soon wake up, another of my dreams.
But suddenly all noise is gone, all once again is still.
I whirl and lying on the ground- my wicked Auntie Lil.
One ghost, no longer bony, but a young and handsome man
Is standing there beside me, shyly offering his hand.
He kisses mine and tells me, "My name is William Blaise."
I was married to your aunt for maybe twenty days.
If any lad had money you could bet that he'd meet Lil.
You couldn't help but love her; this is such a bitter pill.
She's done in all five of us and no one found a thing-
But even for those twenty days I felt just like a king."
Bill ran a misty finger down my reddened cheek.
"You sure do look just like her, Miss, and that's praise I speak.
I heard you met my mother and she gave you quite a scare.
I hope she didn't hurt you, but I'm told she pulled your hair."
I told him weakly, "I'll survive, and I can understand
Why she was so filled with hate, for you're a fine young man.
Yes, I lost some hairs that night, what you heard did occur
Before Aunt Lil turned barber so that I would look like her.
But tell your mother it's all right; that I was never mad.
I wish her a much better rest than these past years she's had."

He whispered something in my ear and I took his advice-
All after Auntie Lil's inquest, which wasn't very nice.
I informed authorities of where Lil's victims lay
Coroners recovered five from Lily's grounds that day;
They determined I was not to blame for poor Lil's broken neck.
I finally left New England, heading west upon my trek.
Kingman, Arizona is where my journey ended
And now I have a fiancé whom I there befriended.
Andy Blaise had lost his wife to cancer years before
Now soon I'll be a mom to his four kids whom I adore.

Oh, I still love the Twenties mood and sure miss Auntie Lil;
I keep my bob and beaded dress with matching slippers still.
But now my life's a happy one and I say with a smile
I'm going to wear Lil's beaded dress when I walk down the aisle.

*

To T.

Like a tree trunk, brutal, strong
A maid might fear you meant her wrong.
One gentle kiss, one tender word
Said I was wrong in what I heard.
Your gruff appearance just façade
A gentle giant, granite hard.
Then I saw your merry smile,
Heard simple words not full of guile,
Your twinkling eyes of truest blue,
What joy I could have known with you!
Before our love could e'er be born
Oh, far too suddenly, you were gone!
Your big, stout heart no longer beating-
Such strong spirit! Why so fleeting?
Buried deep beneath my breast
Your massive form is laid to rest.
Sweet dreams until we meet again;
I'm left behind to dream of then.

*

My Little King

"She wouldn't be my Valentine," poor Jimmy said to me.
He held a box of chocolates unaccepted by Marie,
Some gorgeous, wrapped red roses, a velvet box, a ring.
How could I ever mend the heart of my poor little king?

"I've worked so hard to get ahead, to build us both a life,
I'd waited 'til today to ask Marie to be my wife!
She says I'm too old-fashioned and she won't share my name;
She says to lose her 'big career' would be an awful shame.

She wouldn't take the roses… or the chocolates… or the ring."
Are those tears that fill the eyes of my sweet little king?
A finer, more upstanding boy there simply couldn't be;
A gentle, decent, quiet sort is my son Jim, you see.

I call my boy 'my little king', for that's just what he is.
His friends are all my friends and my friends all are his.
A churchgoing, God-fearing boy, a saint he should be crowned.
His decency must shame Marie. She's jealous, I'll be bound!

But now my little king is sad; I feel his broken heart-
Some snippy girl just took his world and tore it all apart!
How may I mend the pieces and make it right again?
What magic can a mother use to drain her son of pain?

That's when I saw the pistol in the pocket of his suit.
I didn't need to ask him, "Jim, whom do you meant to shoot?"
Broken hearts make broken minds; I let him go his way.
You reporters are the last I want to see today!

*

Tribute to A Drive-In

The making up of sandwiches, the popping of the corn,
Once these things have started, you cannot feel forlorn.
We're going to the Drive-In, going to see fantastic flicks;
We'll see the Great Concession Stand perform its magic tricks.
The hotdogs, hamburgs, popcorn and all kinds of soda pop,
And delicious soft-serve ice cream with some chocolate sauce
on top.
Or maybe try the clamcakes or the spicy onion rings-
You want it? Hey, they've got it! You can buy all kinds of things.
All dressed in our pajamas, we've awaited this all year!
At the big countdown to Showtime we all start to cheer.
Will it be a scary movie or some good old Family Fun?
Or maybe science fiction with a city on the run?
The mini fire engine rides! The kiddie Ferris Wheel!
You just can't beat the Drive-In with its Dollar/Carload deal.
We'll crack the window just enough to fit the speaker in
And in come the mosquitoes, it's a battle you can't win
Unless you buy an insect coil from the concession stand,
But bugs or no, we love it. The experience is grand!
With the family station wagon we would come back faithfully,
And it's a crime this hallowed place is just a memory.
You can keep your DVD's and your home theatres too.

There's only one experience for my buck that will do.
Give me that big blue arrow with all those chaser lights,
Give me the Plainville Drive-In on a Dollar/Carload night.

*

A Safe Haven '71-'74

My Dad said, "Merry Christmas!" back in nineteen-seventy-one
As he gave me a present that has brought me so much fun-
A little red "dice" radio, AM with lousy sound.
I didn't care. For me it was the coolest thing around.
It broke the barrier, introducing me to rock'n'roll,
Before the years of disco when the tunes went down the hole.
The DJ's were like friends to me; I felt I knew them all,
The singers and songwriters, from the greatest to the small.
To eleven-year-old me back then that music was my world;
A safe haven against the pains of adolescent girls.
The music then went downhill and my station went to Talk.
They think that's what I want to hear? Then they can take a walk!
The music is no better now with all sincerity-
How 'bout some tunes with feeling if you're seeking to please me?
Don't need a great big boom box just to make me feel like groovin',
Just a little red dice radio with some sounds to get you movin'.

*

The Legend of Espiritú

I went to visit Amy just before the first of May.
I've never seen San Rafael; it's quite a place, they say.
My cousin lives on Piñon Ranch, that's way up on Red Bluff
Which overlooks the valley, of which I can't get enough.
Amy's like my sister and it really broke my heart
When she met and married Larry, now we live so far apart.
She says she misses Georgia, but not the college life.
Why didn't I come visit her and see a rancher's wife?
Amy's husband Larry sent me pix he took last spring
And asked if I'd come visit them, and I came on the wing.
The one thing that attracted me were stories that they told;

Stories of the West and folklore of the days of old,
Of cowboys and the Indians, the way they lived and fought,
The struggles of the settlers, the little that they brought,
Of bandits and the outlaws, the lawmen on their trail,
The folks who sought their fortunes came by coach or came by rail.
One story that they told me, the one I like the best-
The one about Espiritú, the cave full of unrest.
Anyplace that's haunted always draws me like a fly.
The cave known as Espiritú has caused grown men to cry.
Misfortunes have befallen those who go inside the cave,
And many, far too many, whom it's been too late to save.
Some say there is an angry ghost who guards a cache of gold,
Who'll toss you off a chasm if you come too near, it's told.
Four young men turned outlaw in the year of 'eighty-five;
They robbed the bank and ran to hide; just made it back alive!
They took the gold they'd stolen, to the valley they then flew
And hid it all within the vaults of old Espiritú.
Now many thousand dollars' worth of gold lay in the cave.
To find your way around in there you had to be quite brave.
So many different passage-ways (I hear there's six in all)
With lots of cliffs and drop-offs that could cause you quite a fall.
It's possible to die in there if you are unprepared.
However, those young men got by, whatever way they fared,
They'd still need food just to survive, and still hide from the
law.
Thank God the posse was afraid to approach the cave's great maw.
And so they went to hunt one day for rabbits or for quail.
The sherriff's whose posse sighted them along a brushy trail;
They showered them with bullets, bringing three boys to the ground.
Only one made his escape and him they never found.
He'd run back to his trusted cave and must have bled away;
The ghost and gold are all that's left and they're still there
today.
Oh, other people died there too, folks from the latter day,
They'd hunted gold or souvenirs and fell or lost their way.
Amy told me not to go in any cave alone,
So I just thought I'd go and take a brief look on my own.
I'd just go to the mouth and peek and then I'd walk on by.
What harm could ever come if I stay under open sky?
I hiked from down to the valley and I brought myself a lunch.

Amy loves the desert flowers. I'll pick her a bunch.
And here I am, right at the mouth of that most famous cave;
I'm thinking of that one poor man who made this place his grave.
A lonely death it must have been, a sad one to be sure,
The price for which the outlaw life must have lost its lure.

From the cave a muffled call! I listen once again.
Yes, it's a man. Has he been hurt? I've got to go in then!
"Sarah? Sarah? Is that you? It's Prentice! I'm in here!"
I want to run inside but it's those drop-offs that I fear.
"Hello? Can I help you? Where are you? Are you hurt?"
I call but won't go charging in; with danger I won't flirt.
"Hear my voice and foller it! Stick to the MIDDLE way!"
I plunged ahead and sorely missed the pure, bright light of day.
Three passages diverged and then descended in pitch black.
I didn't bring a flashlight; now there's just no turning back.
Carefully, carefully inching along, I called out to the man,
"Keep talking, now! I can't see much! Guide me if you can!"
The man keeps calling, I keep coming. Is that light I see?
It's flickering- a lantern? It just has to be!
I'm nearly falling headlong; I have to catch myself
Then almost a heart attack from bats along a shelf.
"Hello?" I weakly call again; a cold hand clamps on mine
And pulls me toward a cavern where the flickering lantern shines.
He's just a boy, not twenty-one, and not a handsome lad.
A pointy face, long strawlike hair and Lord, his teeth look bad.
But earnest, questing, sea-blue eyes still pluck at my heart-
strings,
For sometimes beauty misses some of life's most precious things.
He's dressed just like a cowboy with a duster torn and soiled
But when he speaks- sincerity, with manners so unspoiled.
In his thin neck, a gaping wound that should be bleeding free-
It's open and it's ugly but no leakage I can see…
"Why, you're not Anna," he observes. "Did she send you here?"
I struggle now for some response that doesn't sound too queer.
"I don't know any Anna; I thought you called my name.
I'm Sarah- at a distance they both sound so much the same!"
A bashful grin. "I'm sorry, Miss. I brought you down for naught."
I grin right back. "I was afraid that you'd been hurt or caught
Or that you'd fallen down somewhere and maybe broke a bone,

But it seems that you're all right. Are you down here alone?"
"Not anymore, Miss Sarah. You are a welcome sight.
Come let me see your pretty face- come over toward the light.
My name is Prentice Warren and I just turned nineteen.
And even in those trousers, Miss, you sure look like a queen.
I'm waiting for my three best friends; don't think they're comin'
back.
The sheriff's posse caught us out a-huntin' on the track.
No use lyin' to you, Miss, we all four robbed the bank,
We made off with ten sacks of gold, and I got them to thank.
I ain't no robber, that's for certain, just helped out three
friends.
The posse shot 'em up and I guess this is where it ends.
I can't get out, they'll have me trapped, already shot me there."
He probed the hole in his poor neck, which whistled out some air.
"That bled awhile and then it stopped, so I been waitin' here.
Don't know how I'll see Anna." In his eye there welled a tear.
"I did it all for her, you know. We wanted to be married.
How can I bring her gold if to the hangman I am carried?"
It all begins to dawn on me; I start to understand.
I reach out to my friend and ask him kindly, "Take my hand?"
His long and bony fingers have a solidly firm grip.
He's cold, at least not icy, and I chew my bottom lip.
One hundred and nineteen years ago, poor Prentice lost his life
All trying to get some gold so he could make a girl his wife.
This sad and skinny little boy is nothing but a ghost;
His sorrow digs into my heart, and so I pull him close.
"Prentice, you can go now. You've done your time; you're free.
You can go and join your Anna. It's been quite a while, you see.
There's no more posse, no more death, no more feeling pain.
There's no more need for money now, no more pursuing gain.
Just take Anna all your love, that's all that matters now.
She'll be so happy- as I'd be- if you were mine somehow."
"Thank you, Sarah," Prentice mumbles, buried in my hair.
"Lost Anna once; I'm losin' you now- life sure is unfair."
We'll miss each other keenly even after our short time.
I'd touched a piece of history and his story touched mine.
He takes his lantern, leading me down some natural stairs,
Then jerks his thumb somewhere ahead, some dark and dingy lair.
"This is where we kept the gold, right here inside this room."

He hands the lantern to me and points into the gloom.
Prentice gives me one shy kiss and motions me, go on.
I step inside the 'room' but when I turn around, he's gone!
It stuns me for a moment and I feel a pang of sad.
To have him as a friend or more I would have been so glad.
But this is how it's meant to be, he had to move along,
Still in my head a radio plays some sad old cowboy song.
I shine the lantern all around. The light stops on a scene-
A figure slumped against the wall, surrounded, like a queen,
With ten fat sacks of dusty gold just waiting to be found,
My poor, sweet, faithful Prentice guards the gold as he was
bound.
I recognize his boots, his pistol and his bandolier,
Though normally to see a corpse would make me sick with fear.

The bank gave me a fine reward for returning all their gold.
I'm honored that my name is linked to folklore, days of old.
I've had my Prentice buried in the churchyard on the Bluff,
Now he's near his Anna and he'd think that's enough.

I sometimes see him in my dreams, not gaunt, aglow with life!
His deathly pallor gone along with all his earthly strife.
His homely face is beautiful, his happiness complete,
That's just what I want for him- or anyone as sweet.

*

Night Visitor

The thunder rumbled me awake,
All blissful silence did forsake,
Each resonating, throaty snore
I cannot shut out or ignore.
The lightning stabs! It lights my room
And silhouetted in the gloom
He stands there, cloaked, his face obscure-
Not so his purpose; this I'm sure.
Two glowing eyes like red-hot coals,
They pierce the darkness; baleful holes
That lead to Hell! O mortal fear!
His deep bass voice sounds in my ear;

"Come, sweet Madame. Your time is due.
How long have I awaited you!
You've heard that wealth soon comes to dust,
Now keep me company you must.
Mine is your beauty and your youth;
'Tis time to face the awful truth.
You, my debtor, I've come to meet
At your fine home on Golden Street-"
I sat up and with a frown
Said, "Golden Street is two blocks down!"
"Then this is not the DuBois home?"
"Of course not! Out! Leave me alone!"
"My mistake." He's gone from sight
But Eau de Brimstone's here all night.
Why did I ever rent this place
With devils leering in my face?
The Combat Zone's two blocks away-
I'm moving out this very day!

*

The House on Bayley Way

It started when a neighbor child came over once to play
And tumbled down the cellar stairs with gravely-injured head;
Her ghost was seen that very eve just at the end of day,
Just at twilight; then began the legacy of dread.

The Bayley clan was filled with grief at the child's demise.
And later on that Friday their own daughter's arm was gashed.
She'd fallen through a pane of glass and no one heard her cries,
Far too late to save her, they found their own child's arm all
slashed.

The eldest of the Bayley boys died training at West Point
(By now the neighborhood thought this was singular and queer)
The second boy succumbed- tuberculosis of the joint
Which started at his knee and spread its rot up to his ear!

Unable to stand another thing, the missus took her life
(By now none of their neighbor friends would venture near the

place)
Mr. Bayley knotted rope and soon he joined his wife;
The once-respected Bayley clan completely lost their face.

The two surviving Bayleys, brother Kevin, sister Lynne,
Tried valiantly to keep the place and run it best they could;
They both quit school to work full-time and took some boarders in,
But strangers all- what, live in there? No townsfolk ever would.

These boarders soon went packing and the word of mouth spread
'round
That there inside the Bayley house the haunting knew no limit,
That apparitions, poltergeists and spirits did abound
Wreaking mischief in the home and on all living in it.

Even for the family not living there at home
Like Stephen off at West Point, in a fall that snapped his spine
The freakish deaths and happenings began to be well-known.
The selfish neighbors' attitudes were, "Better theirs than mine."

The last two living Bayleys met their end that time next year;
Doctors wouldn't name the cause so who can really tell,
And when the birds were singing and the corn began to ear
The two were found dead in their beds, a sickly yellow Hell.

It's whispered someone burned the place; too many memories
Of sickliness and dying- what a black spot on the town!
The house burned down, that part's a fact, as quickly as you
please,
But in the pile of charred debris, one boarder's corpse was
found.

The stigma of the Bayley place had been the town's one sore;
Its passing seemed to purify. The blight had been knocked out,
The 'curse' was finally broken and would stain the town no more.
The spell of sad misfortune, and of evil, fought its bout.

Spiritualism's Age! Talk to dear, dead Uncle Joe!
If it was your wish the dead could speak at modest fees.
The high-class people of that age, they treat it like a show;
You offer lots of money, you can hear just what you please.

But these were true occurances; the testimonies real
By staunch and good reliable folks with nothing for to gain;
None doubt their integrity, no hoaxes to reveal,
And ever since the house burned down, all's been as right as rain.

The information I've researched is for our family book.
We've built our band new house upon the Bayley house's site;
I'm pasting in some pictures of the old house- have a look!
We'll put it out for all to see- our housewarming's tonight!

We've used the Bayley house's plans; all designs are old and true.
Authenticity's been our rule- a brand new start for Bayley Way!
Our poor Becky can't attend; she's picked up something like the flu.
It's a shame she has to miss our first housewarming day!

(In the American Indian Archives- a curse placed upon that plot
of land by a medicine man of the now-extinct Red Bone Tribe,
1726.)

Once this land tastes fear and death
Its thirst cannot be quenched
You stole from us our very breath
Now deep in blood be drenched!

*

The Black Dove

Today I saw a black dove. Does this mean something bad?
Have we blown all our chances at the peace we've never had?
Is this some kind of warning or was it just a fluke?
Is this a premonition- being laid low with a nuke?
I hope it's just unusual, something born a different way.
For we need no more giant steps en route to judgment day.

*

7/4/04

The sun rises and paints the tops of the trees. Sunday.
Our world is at rest; no dull roar of distant traffic,

Working machinery or people in a hurry. All is picture-perfect!
The summer morning air is alive, fresh and sacred
Just waiting to be tasted.
A church bell calls distantly, reminding us of what day it is.
Our brisk morning walk produces a light sweat,
The birds sing hymns to us and ask for contributions
Of bread or seeds,
And squirrels and chipmunks gossip on their stone wall pews.
Fellowship abounds here as well in a dragonfly perching
On your finger. The bees don't chase, the birds come closer.
Morning dew blesses the grass and the trees
Sweet summer sunshine baptizes us continuously,
A restful peace permeates our spirits-
All are welcome; feel free to worship with us!

*

All Hallows Eve

Bright are the colors of Autumn's shawl
Sparkling, the frost spreads itself over all
From here and from there children answer the call
The call of All Hallows Eve.

The werewolves, the witches, the hissing black cat,
The ghosts and the Frankenstein, mummy and bat
The colors! The parties! The candybags fat
At last it's All Hallows Eve!

Cornstalks of gold, orange gourds piled high
Scarecrows sway 'neath a thunderstorm sky
Sweet treats for the tongue and a feast for the eye
The flavor of All Hallows Eve.

The scent of new costumes from our Five-and-Ten
The glitter and sparkles from our way-back-when
Oh, what I would give to go out again
A child on All Hallows Eve.

And where did it come from, this happy parade
Of pumpkins and candy, this merry charade?

Buried by ages its meaning is laid
The true meaning of All Hallows Eve.

*

Menagerie

Cats and their kittens, foxes and kits,
Charming-eyed mice coyly guarding cheese bits.
Walruses, seals with a white pup or two,
A great white shark with a grin meant for you!
Stallions proud with their mares and their foals,
The white buffalo with her eyes like hot coals.
Woolly-furred poodles of pink, black and white,
A large Spanish bull who's all ready to fight.
A family of chickens, a gaggle of geese,
The ram, ewe and lamb with the snowiest fleece.
Pegasus, unicorns, griffins, a dragon,
A muscular Clydesdale to pull a beer wagon.
Owls horned and barn, snowy, burrowing, screech,
The sow and six piglets, a faucet for each.
A noble blue whale, a beluga, a killer,
A grinning hedgehog and a shy armadiller.
What beautiful collies! A perky Dalmatian
Who begs for a ride to his home fire station.
I love all my pets and add to them each year,
Sensible, whimsical- both bring me cheer.
If you love animals nothing is finer
Than having your own zoo all made of bone china.

*

Pain

Don't deal to me the dreaded blow,
Don't turn your back; I need you so!
You know them all, my secret fears
Don't speak disaster in my ears!
I hurt enough, don't make it worse;
Like being trapped inside a curse.

I've tried to give you happiness
But your warm smiles seem less and less.
Tell me, what more can I do
To make you see my heart is true?
Don't leave me here to die in pain,
But soothe me like a cooling rain.
I've promised not to leave your side,
Your face from me you seem to hide.
I beg you, let my spirit heal,
Your mercy let me finally feel.
Let us now together be,
My love for you and yours for me.

*

Greeting Card

To my good friend who's been such a dear
Here's wishing you joy all the year!
I wish for you daisies and poppies and posies,
Violets, dew-drops and red-blushing rosies,
New-blossomed bluebells, fat gray pussywillows,
Taffy and toffee and mint candy pillows,
Cuddly puppies and fluffy white kittens,
Loppy-eared bunnies with little black mittens-
May all of this sweetness come running your way
To make you feel special this ord'nary day.

(on the inside)

And if by this time you are wrinkling your nose
And feel I'm too mushy with my pretty prose,
Remember I could have asked you to drop dead
Or sent you a letter bomb, dearie, instead.

*

Bead Collection

So cool in my hand, the soft and the loud,
The subdued and the simple, the riotous, proud.

The clay and the wooden, the stone and the glass,
A masterpiece someone produced in a class.
Outer space, deepest ocean both shine at my throat,
The animal patterns, a musical note.
Handpainted, firepolished, the lampwork, dichroics,
The colors of cartoons alongside the stoics.
On the same cord, scorching desert gives way
To silvery rainfall and rainbow display!
The crystals, carnelians, carved bone, amethyst,
Foil-lined cotton candy and peppermint twist.
Rose quartz and cinnabar, mother of pearl,
The jasper and agate, the twisted tube swirl…

I treasure each one and still hoard like a troll
Each like an emotion that colors my soul.
And who will inherit all this when I'm gone?
Who'll string up my feelings and put them all on?

*

Requiem for a Friend

How long ago was it? I can't quite recall.
Old memories play funny tricks, after all.
I still do remember; it's burned in my brain,
Stuck fast like a picture in a scrapbook of pain.
I found him one springtime in the grass 'neath a tree,
Such a sweet, precious creature there never could be.
I raised him by hand, gave him scraps from my plate,
I kept him snug sheltered in a shed by our gate.
Just a plain little bird, never found out what kind,
But the songs that he sang me still haunt my old mind.
If angels can take on a low, earthly form
Then my friend was a seraph whose voice kept me warm.
If I felt my lowest it didn't last long.
My sweet, small companion healed me with his song.
My friends were all envious; they came by to see
My dear little pet when he warbled to me.
Some neighborhood bullies came by one foul night
And snatched up my songbird ere he could take flight,

Mistreated him cruelly then left him for me
On the grass where I'd first seen him under a tree!
I grieved into illness, yet nobody thought
To punish those boys for the crime they had wrought.
"It was only a bird," my friends would all say.
"It's dead. Now forget it and come out to play!
The whole world is out there! The Jazz Age is nigh!
Don't tell us you're just going to sit there and cry!"
Those bullies are dead now and so are my friends
But because they've forgotten, is this where it ends?
Though long ago, my pain is still keen.
Oh, when was it now? It was nineteen-sixteen.

*

Explorer

The stone foundation in the woods
Makes him stop and wonder.
An ancient oak upon the hill,
Corpulent with wisdom
Looks on in silent knowledge
As he pokes about and ponders.
Digging through the pine needles
That form a springy rug,
He spies the rotted floorboards
Just before they plunge him down.
The dutiful pine trees have spread
A fresh, new carpet on the hole,
Undisturbed for fifteen years
While the oak tree still looks on.

I saw this in a dream, you see,
But why should I disturb his tomb?

*

The Blue Blobby Blub

Our Mom made up some gelatin.
It started out like glue,

But when she kept on mixing it
The gelatin turned blue!

It wasn't blue like someone's eyes,
It wasn't blue like sky.
It wasn't pretty, friendly blue
Like Mom's blueberry pie.

This was a sort of scary blue
That didn't look so great.
Then Mom took it to Daddy
And she dumped it on his plate.

"Since when has gelatin been blue?"
Dad asked her with a frown.
"Come on now," answered Mommy,
"Would you like it better brown?"

"No ma'am!" Daddy shook his head.
"The color doesn't matter.
I just don't want to eat that stuff.
Dear, look! It's getting fatter!"

The gelatin began to grow.
It grew to giant size!
As big as our refrigerator
With a pair of eyes!

This wasn't just plain gelatin
To mix up in a tub.
The gelatin had turned into-
A Blue Blobby Blub!

"What is that thing?" cried Mommy.
"How ugly!" shouted Dad.
The monster gulped them down its throat.
It burped and thought, "Not bad!"

The Blobby Blub ate Cissy
And brother Bobby too!
I ran and hid myself away
To see what it would do.

It ate our next door neighbor,
It even ate his wife.
I ran like lightning down our street
And yelled, "Run for your life!"

The monster ate the neighbor's cat
And ate the neighbors' dog!
It even ate the mailman.
The Blub was such a hog!

A policeman saw the Blobby Blub
But couldn't get away.
How much could one monster eat?
Eight people in one day!

At last it wiggled to the woods
To see what it could find.
I hoped it wouldn't see me
As I followed close behind.

The Blobby Blub ate hikers,
A forest ranger too!
That makes eleven people!
Whatever could I do?

The Blobby Blub now spied a wolf
Who looked it in the eye.
Before the Blub could eat him,
The wolf then leaped up high.

He sank his teeth into the Blub
And what do you suppose?
The Blobby Blub, it burst apart!
I got some on my nose.

Out popped Mommy, out popped Dad,
The ranger, dog and cat,
The next door neighbor and his wife,
What do you think of that?

Out came brother Bobby
And sister Cissy too,

Policeman, mailman, hikers now,
All wearing gobs of blue!

"Thank heavens," whispered Mommy.
"Oh, what a fright we've had!"
"Dear, who makes that gelatin?"
Demanded angry Dad.

If your mom makes you gelatin
The box you've got to see.
You must never, never use it
If it says, "B.B.B."

*

Seaplane Ride

It took enough persuading just to get me in his plane.
He knows I don't like flying, thank-you-so-much-just-the-same.
But there I was, all belted in, against my better thoughts.
Takeoffs, landings, turbulence all make me get the trots.

They tie my stomach in a knot and make me want to hurl
The big jet planes are bad enough- no smaller for this girl!
My boyfriend got his pilot's license just a week ago;
Now he feels that all his moves to me he's got to show.

I told him that's how accidents claim more lives every year,
Showing off by brand new pilots, wits not always clear.
Accusing me of gross mistrust, he gets me to agree-
He'll take us in a circle, if that's OK with me.

His seaplane starts to taxi, my stomach starts to twist.
He leans my way, presents his cheek for good luck to be kissed.
And off we go into the sky, onto the Great Big Blue,
If I survive I'll kiss the ground, that's what I'm going to do!

Please wake me when it's over! You got an airsick bag?
I won't ever say these things or he'll think I'm a nag.
We're in the sky, ascending. The view is something grand,
I'd just prefer a mountain view, high up but down on land.

We fly our scheduled circle so high above the lake.
Thank God I see our dock again! A turn he starts to take.
We shudder, shake and shimmy; in the distance I see rain.
Can't you tell how glad I'll be back on the ground again!

At last a bouncy, rough descent. Our engine starts to chug.
Engine trouble? Out of gas? It's in your hands, love-bug!
He spews some words unprintable but steadies us somewhat.
We coast into a landing with our engine's putt-putt-putt.

It's dead. It's stalled. We're coasting now up to our place at
dock.
My loved one looks a little pale, touched by a little shock.
If he touches on the subject of our honeymoon again,
I'll say in no uncertain terms I'm going to take the train.

*

Ballgown

A dream pink and gold trimmed with feathery lace,
All cool, creamy satin and noble brocade,
The bodice boned firmly, so tiny the waist-
Of my fondest wishes this vision is made.
With intricate stitching, embroidery fine,
Besprinkled with rose-colored pearls;
Ribbon blossoms on well-behaved vine,
My bodice's garden unfurls.
To swish and to rustle the skirt sweeps so wide
With soft-padded panniers tied at my hips,
In frill-bedecked underdress, white as a bride,
Trimmed all in rosebuds the shade of my lips!
Securely-tied corset and stockings of silk,
Jewel-dusted pink slippers and handpainted fan,
A feather-plumed hairclip the color of milk,
My cascade of curls, quite the hue of warm sand.
My maids help to dress me; I must take my leave,
To the Queen's spring cotillion I'm bound-
That's when I awaken and then start to grieve;
My dreams once more crash to the ground.
Tied up to machines, not one strand of hair,

No beautiful lady am I.
I cannot get up; why is life so unfair?
No answer- and I start to cry.

*

Artist

His whole front end now new-age sculpture,
Molten copper in his mouth,
In runny pastel colors
His youthful world of promise
Melts before his very eyes.
The modern work of art in crimson
Over silver spiderweb
On the canvas of his windshield-
The sidewalk art he left behind
That police will trace with chalk-
Assures him of his certain fame,
That he will be identified,
This talented young artist,
The one who knocked 'em dead.

*

A Magic Love

A warm and verdant day in spring, my family went away-
We 'crossed the pond' to Britain for a country holiday.
It wasn't for the new 'pop' scene, it wasn't just for kicks
That made us fly to England in the spring of 'sixty-six.
We wanted peace and quiet in a little country inn,
A garden full of flowers far away from London's din.
We found a place called Squire's Rest; it seemed the perfect spot-
Relief from all the school and work that are our daily lot.
An ideal place for writers! Here my ideas could hatch
In this dollhouse of a cottage with its roof all made of thatch.

I wandered through the woods one day to see what was to see,
I'd taken pen and journal too and sat beneath a tree.
For once it wasn't raining; sun was shining, skies were clear,

I'd jotted down a line or two when something caught my ear.
That was when I saw him and at first it caused me fright.
Not since the time I'd seen a ghost was anyone so white!
With eyes of deepest ocean, his countenance so mild,
I knew that he was very old, yet vibrant as a child.
He wasn't tall, but graceful in his stately, silent tread,
Like falling snow his beard and mane adorned his perfect head.
He seemed to smile as he approached and knelt down next to me
And on his forehead, opalline, his spiral ivory.
Like the presence of an angel, he filled me with such peace;
Reborn, renewed, refreshed, reclaimed, rewritten and release!
His skin was not like anything I'd ever touched before-
No suede, silk, satin, velvet ever made me pine for more.
"This isn't real," I told myself. "It can't be, Lord above!
How could plain old me attract this fabled beast of love?
Though this is just a lovely dream, I never want to wake.
If this is just a magic spell then may it never break."
Nowhere have I found such love. No mortal man is able
To make me feel so heaven-blessed as can this precious 'fable.'

My family went back to the States and I remained behind
And to this day I've never breathed a word about my find.
They'd say my writing's got to me; I've finally jumped the track
But would this creature wait until the day that I came back?
So here I've stayed in England fair and I'm still no one's wife,
At fifty-seven, still look eighteen, a magic sort of life!
My friend still feeds me Magic and I weave it into verse;
Soul-mates we shall always be, for better or for worse.

*

Miracle Mirror

I'm looking at the gifts beneath our artificial tree.
They're all wrapped up but I can guess what every one will be.
Some on-sale gaudy makeup, cheap perfume or colored socks,
A sweater I could never wear, some barrettes for my locks,
The latest of computer games, a gift coin, maybe two-
Don't mean to sound ungrateful but my need for this is through.
What's gone out of Christmas? Where is all the love and joy?

What's happened to the happiness inside of one small toy?
This happiest of evenings, why do I shed such tears?
Why is it all so empty now? What's happened through the years?
I heard my parents fighting, must be three days gone by,
All family plans disrupted; Grandma picked that day to die.
She'd sent a present for me and it's standing near the tree...
I wonder if I opened it, if they'd be mad at me.
It's tall and slim, it stands alone, it's covered with a cloth,
What refuse from a junk shop's come to feed our every moth?
Wait! Here's a card addressed to me in small, familiar scrawl;
"Merry Christmas, Jamie dear. I'd wrapped this up last fall.
I knew you'd find this useful, loving antiques as you do,
Old back when Nanna had it, now it's passed to you!
It's not another video, it's no computer game,
But I knew you'd want this gift, for we both feel the same."
An antique full-length mirror, the time frame hard to tell-
That reflection in the glass was not one I knew well.
There was no mirror image; I didn't see my face,
Of the living room in back of me there wasn't any trace...
The room was made of stone, it seemed, as was the fireplace,
The hearth piled high with presents, each one wrapped with old-
world grace.
There hung a heavy chandelier, aglow with dancing flame
Above a massive table piled with dainties and with game;
Seven fat stuffed pigeons, pheasant wrapped in bacon strips,
Coney pie, great wheels of cheese, a dish with metal grips
In which reposed a boar's head garnished well with every spice,
Puddings bursting in their fatness made me want to try a slice.
The table's set for seven, lighted candles everywhere
With holly, ivy, evergreen- I could smell the scent from there!
A windowseat with Christmas crèche with evergreen surrounded,
And all about the room exquisite ornaments abounded.
In the corner- evergreen, though not the modern tree,
Alive, alight, a glorious sight for anyone to see!
Lighted candles sparkle on the garland of glass beads,
More wreath than tree, adrip with colored ornaments it bleeds.
Miniature glass houses, churches, animals and stars,
Flowers, fruits and castles, so much prettier than ours!

Where did Grandma get this? Did she know what it can do?
"We both feel the same," she'd said. I'm sure that Grandma knew.

I stood there, simply gawking at the image in the glass.
If only there were some way, through the mirror, one could pass!
Oh, this was truly Christmas! Nothing tawdry, cheap or fake!
To claim this Christmas scene for mine, what steps would I not
take!
I'm not quite sure what happened next; I guess I dove right
through,
Or else I'd not be standing here and looking out at you.
I'm very sorry, everyone, but I'm not coming back;
I live in Crompton Castle now and nothing shall I lack.
Not Jamie now but Lady Jane, and Grandma's here as well.
Just how we came to be here, how may we ever tell?
Our Christmases shall all be kept as is their proper due,
So from our mirror to the past, Happy Christmas to you.

*

Winter Wizard

He took a winter sunrise, orange, pink and purple-blue,
Adorned with chilly morning stars, one perfect crescent moon;
He cut it out to fit my form, to every curve was true,
Embroidered it with crystal drops, as from icicles hewn.
Like bouffant clouds spread wide the skirt, to rustle, softly
sway,
With snowflake-pattern lacy trim and Jack Frost-feathers sewn.
Bejewelled with sleety diamonds in their wintry array,
He made for me the finest dress a daughter's ever known.

*

A Haiku

One day of full sun
Followed by a year of rain-
To be without you.

*

Visionary

I visited my daughter's house in August of that year,
Not one for premonitions or for silly flights of fear.
I tell you with all honesty and look you in the eye,
The things I saw that August were enough to make me cry.

That night I left, walked down the street and turned the corner there,
And felt a chill impossible for the sweltering evening air-
I turned and saw my daughter's house, top story all aflame!
You know I'm no spring chicken, but I raced back just the same.

I had to get the family out! They're nowhere in the yard!
To hear the roar of flames that big could scarcely be called hard.
My daughter must have thought me mad for making such a fuss;
"Why there's no fire, Mother. Why must you frighten us?"

She spoke the truth, for all was well. The upstairs looked just fine.
There was no trace of flame or harm, of smoke there was no sign.
You can bet that I felt foolish. No, I never touch a drop!
This time I would head home to bed and this time I won't stop.

But stop I did; I turned around and there it was once more-
The windows belching smoke and flame, confined to their top floor!
The roar! The sparks! This was no dream! I ran back once again,
But when I burst into the house, things were no different then.

The upstairs of the house was fine without a trace of fire.
A visit to the doctor may be just what I require!
I must be suffering from the heat, decided my good daughter,
And she sent me to the kitchen for a pitcher of ice water.

Her summer kitchen wasn't lit, but cooling was the gloom;
But I was not alone in there, for floating in the room
Came a child's white coffin moving slowly through the air
To stop before the window, where it stayed, suspended there.

All that was many years ago, the coffin, phantom fire,
But anyone who knows me knows I've never been a liar.

That house is now a funeral home, and I learned recently
The kitchen's now the coffin room; so what was wrong with me?

*

Teacher, or The Silver Dragon

O patient eyes of sapphire blue
Reflect the knowledge passed to you
By sage long nameless, long forgotten,
Immemorially begotten.
No crumbling scrolls, no dusty racks
Of tomes to rot in musty stacks;
Your instruction is your word,
Your language few have ever heard.
Your school of singularities
Revealed impossible mysteries;
How may my spirit give off light,
My human body sustain flight,
Another's heart my eyes may read,
I to another's thoughts pay heed,
How may I understand the words
Of beasts, leviathans to birds,
To read the sky, to bring a rain,
To heal both injury and pain,
How to, with song, make flowers bloom
To dispel winter's icy gloom,
To muster superhuman strength,
Extend life to incredible length,
To work great good with heart aglow,
Spread gladness everywhere I go.
My teacher, heartfelt thanks I give
For showing me the way to live.
You taught me to dispel the tears,
The burden of a thousand years.
How many present 'heroes' may
Lay claim this unbelieving day
To a teacher such as you
With ancient eyes of glorious blue?
Who believes in Dragonkind

Who prides themselves on modern mind?
Great Silver Dragon, Trillaley,
Live forever and a day!

*

State Hospital

Rusty metal railings, a draft runs through each room,
The rotting roof sports gaping holes, air musty as a tomb.
Your hollow footsteps scare some birds who burst from unseen
nest,
This is the perfect place to put the squeamish to the test.

There's plenty of equipment that people left behind;
Gurneys, tables, cabinets, the handrails for the blind,
Electro-shock equipment, beds and gurneys with restraints,
Fire hoses for the folks who caused the staff complaints.

There are bars on lots of windows for the criminally insane;
You can feel where people suffered; many rooms still reek of
pain!
There's still a cafeteria, a bowling alley too-
A recreation room where there were happy things to do.

But worst of all, the tunnel- from one building to the next
So people won't be forced to see the patients and be vexed.
The loud, the unpredictable, the vile and the obscene
Went through this passage underground so they could not be seen.

Folks say this place is haunted and you believe it's true.
They say that blood still stains the walls and some equipment too.
You know you've got to see it- till someone grabs your arm!
The cop growls, "Nothing works here but our Trespasser Alarm!"

*

Typhoon

Into our midst she rages
All clad in icy blue,
A gown of wrinkled satin

And ragged, frothy gauze.
Cool dignity forgotten,
She slams the innocent sands
To breach the sea wall
And vent her rage upon us.

She screams about the oil slicks
While overturning ships,
She blames us for the death of whales
And crushes hapless homes.
For us, a better thing by far
Is not to disagree.
We let her vent her anger
And satisfied, flounce away.

*

Kerri's Tale

My second- best friend Amber called me on the phone last night
To ask me to sleep over now that school is finally done,
With take-out food from Whiffy's we could do it up all right
Add a couple of our other friends, we'd have ourselves some fun!

Amber's grandma lived here once. It's whispered she had powers…
A psychic/gypsy/sorceress who woke the spirit world,
Back and forth she'd rock and grunt and moan and shake for hours
Though that was many years ago when she was just a girl.

You know the way it often is to sleep in some strange bed;
You get someone's unfinished dreams, or you can't sleep at all.
I must admit I had the creeps, those stories in my head;
I'd drown them with some Cherry-Aid! And tiptoed down the hall.

I crept down toward the kitchen, headed through the living room
And saw a figure near the couch. My God, I'm not alone-
A dark-cloaked creature stared at me, eyes piercing through the gloom,
A face too horrid to describe which froze me to the bone!

"Eldora," croaked the awful Thing, who slowly moved my way.
At first I couldn't even budge. What would it do to me?

It smelled half like a toilet and half like dead decay-
I bolted out into the snow and fell and skinned my knee.

Wearing just my new pajamas, wild of hair and bare of feet
I'd pelted home, three blocks in all, a record for thirteen.
Never felt the icy puddles, never felt the stinging sleet,
My parents don't believe me; they just think I'm being mean!

They think I fought with Amber then invented this whole tale!
Eldora was her grandma's name, I found that out today,
And what about those sooty prints and stench that's going stale?
Please, Doctor, tell me you believe and send me home to stay!

*

He Who Runs Like Wind

We met in Gray Rock Canyon
Two cool springs ago.
His gold-green eyes were curious
As I sat to braid my hair.
He did not offer to attack,
Nor has he ever since,
And since that day he follows me
And keeps me in his sight.
Grandfather blessed our friendship
Saying, "He-Who-Runs-Like-Wind
Is guardian spirit to your heart.
Child, look to him and learn."
Policemen know not spirit-guides;
They gunned him down today,
Said cougars are a danger
And broke our sacred bond.
That is why my blood flows free
On stones where we have walked.
Three golden brothers from his tribe
Surround me as I leave.
Run swiftly, brothers, to the hills
Before they come for you.

*

Nanna Banana's Ice Cream

Welcome, big and little shavers, to my house of many flavors!
Here you'll find the greatest ice cream in the world!
Before you say you'll buy it, why not come on up and try it?
We've got something here for every boy and girl!
We've got peanut butter brickle, peachy apple, lemon prickle,
Chocolate-coconut-banana-pink surprise!
Blueberry-orange spicey, cherry-nilla-berry icey,
We invent new flavors right before your eyes!
Chocolate-hazelnut-raspberry, peppermint-and-cherry-merry,
Yummy butterscotch and marshmallow supreme,
Pow-pow punch and buttercrunchy, lime 'n' almond mango munchy,
We can satisfy your wildest ice cream dream!
Java-fudgy-cocoa-toffee, mocha buzzy-wuzzy coffee,
Bubblegummy-taffy-pineapple parfait,
Calling all you flavor-cravers, do yourself a big fat favor-
Visit Nana's crazy ice cream shop today!

*

Fairy Godmother

From fairy mist and angel satin, elvish lace and dragon's silk
From mermaids' pearls and dwarvish gems, wizards' crystals and
their ilk

No regard for wind or weather
Just as light as any feather
How I wove them all together
With my wand as white as milk.

A fan that tinkles when it flutters, icy slippers made from glass
Enchanted opals in the necklace, emeralds green as springtime grass

When the midnight stroke is sounding,
Farewell, prince's arms surrounding,
From the ballroom she'll come bounding,
Til magic once more comes to pass.

*

Payback Day

One night he walked up Thayer Street
Toward his old neighborhood
A visit to his childhood friend
Could only do him good.

He walked past their old playground
Where they spent so many hours,
He passed the hill where they would go
To pick their mothers flowers.

He saw the rotting tree fort
Where on that fatal day
His childhood sweetheart shoved him off
And put him in this way.

All that was twenty years ago
That day with Sharrie Jones,
There wasn't too much left of him
To cling to dirty bones.

His head, it still lolled drunkenly;
The fall had snapped his neck.
But he would find his Sharrie
And set things right, by heck.

*

Bury St. Edmunds

My eyes bear silent witness to the evils of the years,
Squeeze shut and shed their bitterness in needling, stinging
tears.
This place should still be living, any place so fair and sweet;
Its hallowed confines echoing with worshipful, soft feet,
The silky sound of whispered prayers, the flick'ring candle flame,
The grandeur of this building puts the modern kind to shame.
The evil men have come and gone who laid this place to waste;
Imagine now their terror at the wrath upon His face!

I pray that up in Heaven a similar place does stand
Unbound by earthly limits, quite a thousand times as grand!
For Progress and Modernity must for their sins atone
And what we call The Real World is still not carved in stone.

*